THE GATE OF HORN

THE GATE
OF HORN

POEMS

L. S. ASEKOFF

TRIQUARTERLY BOOKS

NORTHWESTERN UNIVERSITY PRESS

EVANSTON, ILLINOIS

TriQuarterly Books
Northwestern University Press
www.nupress.northwestern.edu

Copyright © 2010 by L. S. Asekoff. Published 2010 by TriQuarterly Books/Northwestern University Press. All rights reserved.

Printed in the United States of America

10 9 8 7 6 5 4 3 2 1

Library of Congress Cataloging-in-Publication Data

Asekoff, L. S. (Louis S.), 1939–
    The gate of horn : poems / L. S. Asekoff.
      p. cm.
    Includes bibliographical references.
    ISBN 978-0-8101-5212-0 (pbk. : alk. paper)
    I. Title.
PS3551.S334G38 2010
811'.54—dc22

2009043323

∞ The paper used in this publication meets the minimum requirements of the American National Standard for Information Sciences—Permanence of Paper for Printed Library Materials, ANSI Z39.48-1992.

This book is dedicated to Louise Kalin.

CONTENTS

ACKNOWLEDGMENTS

Grateful acknowledgment is made to the editors of the following publications, in which these poems first appeared:

Alaska Quarterly Review: "Ghost Warrior"

The American Poetry Review: "The Keeper of Records," "Melanoma," "Soliton," "Sparrow," "The Waters of Time"

Boston Review: "Dies Irae"

The Brooklyn Rail: "Levi's Straus"

The Brooklyn Review: "House of the Fifth Sun," "The Widows of Gravesend"

The New Yorker: "Black Valentine," "The Gate of Horn"

Ninth Letter: "Farrago," "Fugue"

Princeton University Library Chronicle: "Shoah"

The Recorder: "Oracle"

Poets Against War Website: "Empathy"

Slate: "The Conquerors"

TriQuarterly: "H*t*l M*rq**s"

I am deeply indebted to my first readers: Eamon Grennan, Robert Hamburger, Kathleen Hill, and Carole Maso.

THE GATE OF HORN

BLACK VALENTINE

Passing through the Gates of Life
I heard the secrets women whisper
Only to women: the rhythms of
His winter-long depressions, manic springs—
Drawn shades, bleeding blue willowware plates,
The hidden photo of his father, a darkly debonair mustachioed
       Russian shoemaker
Angrily hammering nails along the Androscoggin,
The dented silver hairbrush he never let her touch.
With my sister she unties the love knot—a suicide note
In a locked box, confesses the rape
In the North End stairwell when she was eight,
While with me she recalls again & again
The unlikely miracle of my birth,
How I rose that December morning from her once-shattered pelvis,
"A blue-eyed Dresden doll."

THE WIDOWS OF GRAVESEND

It is told & it is told & it is told again.
Whispered in the kitchen by women
dividing violets,
separating beans from stones.
There came a man then
walking in his father's shoes
who heard the three dogs barking by the stream
& at the crossroads
owned neither by this woman nor that man
saw two white horses in a line
& said, "Yes, I am a wanderer in my own land."

Who are you anyway?
An old crow fallen among gold apples?
A man shaving his father's face in the mirror?
Naked under the white sow of the moon
with only the fakebook of Beauty for feeling,
you think, What is my life?
A dog abandoned at the end of summer?
A walk in the rain?
I have lived with my body so long, is it not my soul?

Sadness tunes the instrument.
There is a chill on everything.
You feel the surge, the violent momentum of
emptiness filling immense forms,
energy frozen in each cell,
the snowplow in a sea of waves spellbound by starlight.

Night, night,
sweetest sister, weary river flowing on,
who will sing all our tomorrows?
The lucky ones who continue to live having nothing?

"THE WATERS OF TIME"

& who will paint the great sea within us?
The stone carver? The women who write in water & silk?
The invisible white bees of eternity?
The eye in the womb?
Through the arches of time the water flows backward
& you wake from mirthful & darkly humorous sexual dreams,
naked, wrestling with the bearded man
before the gnarled, tangled roots of the olive tree
amid wild waves, swirling whitebacks of ancient Lesbos,
a coiled ocean foaming with shattered rose petals, pink trembling women.
You laugh out loud at life's excess, its overspill, perverse energy.
No Ithaka but this, you say.
Harbored in the sailcloth sheets of the four-poster bed,
you can smell warm bread in the oven, the distant scent of apples &
       Jamaica Blue Mountain coffee.
Beyond the pale veil a red house is burning.
In milky first morning light, a face floats on the surface of a spoon,
       sky-blue eyes & *Toura loura loura,*
& below, the deep silences of he whose only gifts are the black book,
       carved meerschaum,
& the wish you had never been born.
Shaving before the mirror, razor in hand, face half lathered, you hear
       the phone ring,
freeze as the electric surf of the tape plays out the gutturals
       of the long-forgotten voice,
insistent, German, urgent.

MELANOMA

for E.G.

After the freezing, the incision, the five stitches,
you walk out of the sun where the flag iris, the gold sails of the daffodils
tremble in late May wind. Three lavender tulips, blowsy, overblown,
lean against a stone wall like absinthe drinkers at a Paris bar.
You point to a patch of gravel below us where a heroic brown ant—
farm tractor, armored warrior—lugs behind him
the corpse of a honeybee twenty times his own weight
& marvel at the microscopic power of the barely visible.
"It's no bigger than a pinprick," you say. "They'll know
        for sure in a week.
If it's what he thinks it is, they'll have to take a big chunk out of me."
Measuring the mortally beautiful Greek word on your tongue,
you stare down at the crater where Achilles drags Hector,
the terrible burden shouldered, into the lengthening blue shade of the iris.

SPARROW

People are predators
They can smell mother-love on you just like animals & they keep away
It protects you even as it eats you alive—
The mother-with-claws
We're wired for distance as a species that's how we survive
I'm not talking about copycat language of the oppressed
But the *speed* of language between mother-child
Sparrow sparrow little sparrow
My mother's breasts are eyes—watching me watching me
Father was the raven in the white nightshirt
He could name anything—a conquistador in snow
His motto: *Navigare necesse est . . .*

Listen this island is full of voices
They talk & talk
They put holes in each other
They fill each other with holes
They stand in pools of light of time
They look like their fathers when they are young
Like their mothers as they grow older
Wave the wand & there are pictures in the air
I remember the sea & the sky
A triangle a pyramid beside the sea
I remember the carpenter drew a missing leg—the hypotenuse
Where is the child?
The child *is* the shepherd
Parents are sheep

The man I married was a smooth one
He took me across the waters
Feel your contradiction he said
I need to roll my tongue before I talk to him
His voice is in my head
& he won't listen to what I learned from pain
I'm not lecturing you I said
It's not in my Buddha nature
But I know what language is
Language is an occupying army
& money? Money is a gun
You cash it in for shame & sorrow

After he came back
He attacked me with anger & an army
Verbal abuse they call it
You're no nomad I say
You need someone to make your bed cut your hair
You have to decide where your home is
You can't spend your whole life fixing clocks changing lightbulbs
Why is it I say when men come home from the war
They can't hold their babies?

We've reached a point of no return—like a black hole
Call waiting & it's his crazy brother
Screaming blue murder from Bellevue
& there's the doctor on the phone
I don't need this I tell him
I'm not the closest living relative
I learned my language from conquerors kings
A stranger child walking barefoot in snow
& last month I missed my period

That family they're all talking people—huffing & puffing
Oh I know they won't kill me
I have friends who smile as I walk by
They say my name
Sparrow little sparrow
I've been in this country how long ten years?

FUGUE

I

From ridiculous heights of tulip mania
to icy catastrophe of the falls
down treacherous steps
of the bravely deciduous
"I am alone in my head"
balances off
"You make the body almost profound."

A turbulent system hanging in air,
papery wasp nest, beehive
hairdo, static
cyclone of
the pinecone's whirl-
pool tourbillion
spiraling to
the eye of the storm . . .

Now above quivering stalks,
the pellucid blue
& darkly-purple-belled delphiniums,
whir of invisible wings,
the hummingbird's iridescent
thimbleful of energy,
vibrant tuning fork of light,
that ruby-gorged
cloisonné & clockwork marvel,

jeweled heart of an electron orbiting its shell,
darting, hovering, wavers an instant,
all stasis in motion,
dips hypodermic beak
into honeyed well of morning,
once, twice,
then veering—gone,
as you think,
When you're in love, you're inside the flower!

II

Out of breath
you have fashioned this house
& it holds you, a moment,
the thing uncalled for,
its palest tracings.
Time here is a measure of the genius loci.
Taupe-colored cumuli sail by the window.
Ghostly neutrinos stream through cloud chambers, iron mountains.

**"If this train is visible again,
it may occur in evening twilight . . .
Watch for streaks of light
seeming to have an origin near the double cluster.
Do not look there, however,
because the chunk is headed right for the viewer.
(It won't get there, though, because . . .)"**

& now the phone rings:
Do you know who this is?
This is God in Hell
(My first grade teacher was Miss Nethercoat.)

I was the one who left you the felt-tip pen,
inscribed, in gold:
"The world as I found it."
Though you recognize the urgent pain of a stranger
(darkly luminous as the chrysanthemums of Puccini),
in this place where silence cups its palms
you gather the grains one by one,
reciting your mantra:
I write to remember I write to forget.

III

You go down in robe & slippers to the damp cellar
stare by flashlight at the rusted box—
ceramic & brass fittings,
milky eye of the blown fuse,
a cataract under green glass.
As you screw in the new one
you feel the vibrating cord, swift current,
frozen translucence of sheaves of white crocuses,
dark gladiolas shining through snow,
hiss of fissures in huge blocks of iced moonlight,
rose-pink flesh of silver-foil trout in the freezer tray,
& now eyes closed, you are numb & singing,
dancing wildly in the tingling flow,
a shipwrecked horse,
bottled lightning,
flurry of thunderstruck crows.
You can hear the rustle, distant flutter,
electric hum of black metal fan in a hotel room in Bangkok,
as they glide toward you in soft-soled slippers,
the flower-shirted Laotian houseboys, dreaming of death.

IV

Pinned to the wall,
wave-sections, Hokusai rocks,
a jade & meerschaum sea churning, churning
with liquid mimicry of a baby, its learning in overdrive,
Leonardo's two views of a bare-breasted woman,
exhausted, ecstatic,
devoured by the cannibal she's nursing,
& the man with four arms, legs whirling in his fiery wheel.

On-screen a jittery pen
traces jagged peaks & valleys,
tremors, aftershocks of the heart-stopping terror
that swims into view—
Shining Path, Blue Pavilion, Army of God, Aum Shinrikyo—
firestorm sweeping East like leaves in a jet stream,
random free fall through mirroring markets
as you write, *Those who lie down with owls wake beside lions.*
Our darkness is their dawn.

As you type code for
the slim stems of
these transparent iris
unfurling
papery parasols for
the shadow geisha of Hiroshima,
your e-mail reads, *Let Besso's roses bloom*
as you continue your infernal journey
on Mach's little horse
through the quanta, the relativities
& deadly Amanita, pale mushroom, destroying angel . . .

V

He sits at the desk with sheets of paper & his Waterman pen.
He is revising *Pictures from the Water Trade*.
Through the rice-paper shade,
the weak lightbulb glows,
a goldfish swimming in a cloudy bowl.
The eye follows the hand,
its loops & serifs,
scriven signs of quick things—shadowy
skia, the squirrel,
swirls of jet & ermine,
paw prints in snow,
& crowning it all,
Zen master stroke,
plunge of ink-laden brush on to unmarked paper,
shodo, the Way of Writing—
three samurai,
giant black chrysanthemums,
folded in upon themselves,
explode into space—supernovae.

Before stepping out into the noon sun,
he puts on his white shirt, white pants, white shoes, white hat,
thinking, *I am becoming invisible to myself.*

CODA

Dear L & L,
Boats beached. White whale elusive, submerged beneath
polar cap. Still in pursuit. Have taken to the dogs. Siren song
frozen in crystal melody compelling. Invitations to stay.
Have to confront pervasive disorder & latent sorrow.

Work on strength of loneliness. So difficult to allow affection, desire, to stir up emotions. Snow swirls around me, quick-frozen quanta, silver fireflies, anointing my brow. A world of waves, particles, freaky equations. People believe in mystical laws. They say there is a divine purpose in my being here. I reply: It's all fortuitous. I move as a prime mover. In a circle? Gravity must soon bring me down to earth.

Love, Ahab (*"Schwarzchild"*) Dzous

PS. Meditating on my singularity. Strange attractors. Self-avoiding random walks. Bilocating now. Perils of Pauli! (Do I Bohr you? *Ha-ha!*) Diesels churning, pistons popping, glide into Oslofjord. Sporting a beard. Will I pass for black sheep? Under the midnight sun shall I see things more clearly?

FARRAGO: AN ARIA

O, you are sad, sad.
Get a black dog & sing to it.
Get a black dog & sing to it, I say.
Here the daffodils are in bloom & everyone, absolutely everyone
        is speaking Italian.
No, no woman was ever so loved
& then came the sweet entreaties, hushed money, lushest honey
        glistening on a knife!
These days he flies over mountains of green salt
while I sit beside the window with its fading paperwhites
& no one, I tell you, no one is counting the losses.
Neither the aviator with the White Owl in his mouth
nor the retired sea captain who nurses the bottle.

How then stop the spiral, the roll
of the railroad, workhorse sentences
whose double entries reveal *porto escondito,* borderline disorders,
the avant-garde miracle of everyday life?
I ask you, Can a gentile copy the Torah?
Open the black box of the dictionary to its shining letter *E*?
Just because you're sober, I said, *doesn't mean everything's roses.*
First free the hand, he replied, *then the world.*

I agree "In the maternity ward of the stars
the Unknown is born out of Nothing."
No *is* the mother of Yes,
& yet nothing can explain runaway sexual selection,
the sun's slight preference for red,

the tyranny of outcomes that leads us to
radiator as wings, clockwork cicadas, locusts in their primes,
the inventor of tone rows fear of thirteen.
Under the azure dome
"the inexplicable absence of birds"
sends us spinning toward a spherical shell
where the angelic choir, quivering, sings—atoms on the head of a pin.

Yes, looking back from here, objects are closer than they appear.
My first memory was of women & of water,
open systems of cloud & flame,
fantastic flowers breathing space & time
as non sequiturs of smoke
trail into thinning ozone where
on the other side of breath
they hazily float—lavender & indigo & black . . .
Indeed, whether you are a passenger in someone else's dream
or a prisoner of your own neurosis (viz., electrolysis, travel)
makes no difference to the guttural thunder of a train
steaming beside a river of melting ice
& even the plasterer on the blue bicycle speeding toward you
with his bucket of archaic roses knows
while grief is cut from a single cloth, joy comes in all its motley.

What are these passing shadows?
Hammers of light? White raven wings?
Shards of brightness? Shatterings?
Heaven's hive of albino bees?
Black tulips raised by Baron Samedi, your lover?
O, who hung the moon in the sky?
Rose thrice from the ashes?

No, it was not always easy being the Dakota's
greatest living diva. Going through the motions
I would watch him weave out of water & of wind

across the luminous air
this island's music & its voices.
Limping like an angel across stately erasures of time
he'd plant a kiss, a bruised apricot,
on my chocolate-gloved palm & lisp, *Farrago,*
our love is like two Jews in Germany,
connoisseurs of grief comparing pain.
Together we wept for the rain forests of Brazil,
Brancuşi's falling dog, Humboldt's marvelous bird,
the blind woman's photographs,
all the sad inventions—mousetrap, hair museum, gold tooth mountain,
chicken bones thrust through bars,
the black factory where the mad astronomer
practices long division against the night,
brave souvenirs of those who stood in lonely solidarity with the weather
& died in defense of the rain.

Blossoming out of the sleeve of time
one by one they fall from the sky—milkweed puffs,
breath on a mirror. Uncocooned
one crashes through the roof of our observatory garden,
all pussy willow splendor & pitchfork fury—
Prince Alexei, the aviator,
daredevil nephew to the radiant Curies.
It was, as they say, a spit & dive operation,
entering the White City after dark,
pulling the shade on the sun,
knowing all the while after the Great Forgetting comes
the stranger we must pay for with our lives.
One of those moments in the history of the West
when all the violins are weeping
& as perspective dwindles under our wing
to grains in a cup, poison pearls of the Lesser Antilles,
trapped between a slow pulse & a maniac heartbeat,

l'idée fixe of velocity frozen in a Testarossa's rearview mirror
& the mesmerizing stillness of the snub-nosed Italian revolver
pulled from his pocket, he stares down its muzzle,
& sighs, *My black-eyed beauty . . .*

Herr Doktor Doppler,
whether you *blew* my mind or *read* my mind,
as the wave collapsed back upon itself
I knew I was a victim of these beautiful misreadings—
"rain on silver stilts," "Adam's myth," "the mishearing of sheep in Australia,"
the true *cauchemar* on the aubergine couch.
Psychoanalysis, the Baron hissed,
the shameful spectacle of a child abusing its parent!
Yet who does not want reparations for his childhood?
O, shadow of melancholy in the garden,
as the illusory arrow speeds backward toward its naked singularity,
Mira, the Wonder Star, signals from the tail of the Whale!

My darling, the Baron said, *if there is a geometry of hope,*
there is also a mathematics of despair.
& in the heat of the moment,
when, as they say, things come to a head
or, in the alchemy of desire, grow to a foot,
what of it? No one counts coincident inches!
Yes, the last act is tragic,
yet in the final hours we bravely play piquet
with our executioners, cursing the light,
making idols of the darkness . . .
Death, he laughed, *is a joke only Life can tell.*
& Hell is consciousness of Time in Eternity!

Son of Eros, I sang,
all the sore losers.
I am Rrrrrose of the Levee,

a woman spawned
by the daughter of a woman
scorned by swans—
Anemone,
naked wave-walker
echoing a sky,
weaving from ill wind
& dialectics
the dress of departures.
Hostage to thieves of fire
& smoky interludes of the stone lute,
I followed the candled feet of the sisters of Silence & Old Time . . .
Dim memories persist—horseshit
& how to milk a cow,
leaf-fire on frozen water,
icy yellow iris light,
& the sun a blue mess of meat on the floor.
I was burning, burning on that bed.
I was on fire!
I want gravity & grace! I cried.
Over & over I died with his name on my lips.
The shine went out of everything.
Yes, I am one of those who have felt death toss them in the air
& landing precisely on the point of pain
continued dancing posthumously beyond themselves
to the window that opens to Three Weathers
& saw the wish that denies itself—desire—a delay in glass . . .

I am writing you now from bluest Bruges,
city of glazed light & stones
where a man with white eyes reads Babylonian nights, ancient weathers.
Over a fiery lake of flowers
I taste last night's ashes on my tongue,
memoirs of motor cars & ormolu mirrors

suspended above a green wicker cage & swooning couch
where the man in black opera hat says,
I am gathering pearls for the greater glory of the Lord.
You are converting sea fog into drinking water.
Looking up from a showers of sparks in the breezeway,
the other one says, *After everything fell apart,*
I became a night watchman, a Burns detective,
flew for Blackbird Airlines, the arsonist's crow.
I understood my life in terms of
failed marriages, broken machinery.
With one polished boot on the parapet,
he raises his glass to the first champagne star
& toasts, in perfect French: *Let us drink*
to the pilots in search of lost weather.
For where the snail is only a mountain in motion
the man with the long pole shakes the sky!

SOLITON

If to question the Ukrainian beekeeping academy
is to question
the fate of the empire,
who dares ask for the absent barber,
the right hand of Billy Aalto,
the smashed glasses of Huang Bin Tho?
Tonight they are running rats on rue de Rivoli.
The hydrangea scuds through low clouds.
World, world!
The obol-eyed clerk,
the blind philosopher hugging a horse
suspect the living of being
a rare species of the dead.
Between the inkwell & the stars,
the empty spaces remind us
of what is not there.
Flying solo above the flames
you see the future
fan out before you as
one by one you discard the cards in your hand.
You say, I will never reach the peaks of Machu Picchu,
eat starfish on the beaches of Brazil,
sleep where grosbeaks gather for their nests
pieces of evening.
I am tired of sitting at the edge of the bed
watching my fingernails grow,
staring down at those startling little immortelles,
fish-eye tapioca,

swimming on the cruel plate,
feeding pepperoni to the starlings.
I cannot remember the Czarina, my mother.
Lifted by "the jaws of life"
out of the moaning ocean,
the sucking hole,
I heard winches squeal, harnesses creak
as the black stallion plunged
through the fiery facade.
A voice said,
Whether you sing, whether you sign,
I have given you the animating principles,
shown you the numbers & the stones.
At least learn to love
the one that brought you.
Here, Chinese gentlemen say good night to the trees.
Women bleed involuntarily under the moon.

II

DIES IRAE

A tinny Angelus rings in your ear.
Is this the message from the Great Unknown?
A secret raven? A red sky? Signs of the times?
The "dark place" where most people don't want to go?
Or are they merely selling the weather?
Wreathed in sea smoke, Leukothea, the white goddess,
speaks to you (in archaic Greek) of calculus,
the "lack" in lilac, lyrical blue milk of the mother.
"A hand passes over flowing water," she says,
"you are moved by your motion.
Yet only the gold string knows where it is going."
& looking up from his book, the counting master replies,
"The sleepmaker listens for a foot on the stairs.
O, Jews of One Lemon, Nothing can save you."

While schooling, like mass hysteria, has its advantages
as the full moon rises over the spawn,
all the losses begin rolling in—bright spaces of absence,
& that metal taste under the tongue,
an obol for the ferryman, interpreter of silences.
Wandering calendar, angry river,
I know "No one goes out to buy zero fish,"
yet if we lift the veil & look beneath
we see amphibian ghosts, departed quantities,
insistent whispering of infinitesimals & echoing back to us
"Time like an ever-rolling stream . . ."

What stirs? Where did you go? How do men bear it?
We do not know. Cursed till the god come,
we wager a penny for a bushel of wheat, a penny for
three bushels of barley, wait with the reckoner of lines
for the knock at the door. No doubt each of us
has stroked the sooty black cock in the dark room,
entertained an angel unawares.
Who has clean hands? The gloved guardian stealing from his ward?
Under the bright cloak, we are all thieves.
A white cuff shoots from a sleeve;
the whirring machine factors equations to nothing.

In our reveries our bodies strike us
as the periphery of a circle whose center is "*i.*"
Served & severed, the little soul wavers—
animula vagula blandula—&
we bear a message we cannot read.
Each night in sleep the ship that carries us
is pulled apart, peg by peg, & every waking day rebuilt
out of new matter in the old form. Always arriving,
we go on & on with our ghostly cargo,
our thin, cold minds receptive as snow . . .

ORACLE

Home from the mines of Hebei,
Wei Jingsheng,
his scalded eye &
toothless mullet grin.
He who saw "the dark face of the State,"
tasted ash from the bitterest star,
reads ideograms off butterfly wings,
hears the jade battalions of the waves shattering on sand,
bows before the Emperor of Salt—
a cod's head, its corona of flies.

EMPATHY

In the Dream of Almost-Perfect-Peace,
you wave out the window to your enemy,
who looks up from his cup of coffee, the blue flicker
      of morning news,
to cautiously wave back at you & smile.
There's a strangely familiar scent in the air—
oranges? oleander? myrrh?—
just before the laser crosshairs home in on
the white towers of his city,
wiping him out in the screen's green glare.
Yes, we are all brothers
under the well-oiled wheel of Empire,
& both feel the spear—he, the shock of the sharp edge
      piercing his innocent side,
& you, the shiver of the shaft vibrating back through
      your equally innocent hand.

THE CONQUERORS

They showed us the white flower of surrender
They showed us the red
They fell down before us at the gates of their city
Terrible to behold we hovered above them
Lords of the Air
We promised them the peace
That passeth all understanding
We promised them the freedom of the broken knee
Only the conquered can know
Rumors arose strange premonitions
A talking fish a white crow
& news of uprisings in the distant provinces
Trouble closer to home
Victims killing victims a priest cried
Who is blameless?
The Lords of the Air who dare not touch earth?
Those who kill without risking death?
Following the itinerary of stars
We returned to our city
There we found they had raised in our absence
At the center of the great walled marketplace
A statue of Phobus
God of Fear
As they fell down before us
Perhaps we can be forgiven for asking
Having lived so long among strangers
What is there to fear?

HOUSE OF THE FIFTH SUN

AZTLÁN

Place of Whiteness
"Rising out of the lake like a dream"

Stone gardens
Floating geometry of pyramids

Shimmering in the light of the fifth, the last sun

& beyond the mist
Echoes of a sea

Saltpeople farming the shores of evening

TOLTEC

Once they wrote with flowers
Once invented what they made
Once all precious things were one
Once they walked in skyblue sandals
Among the light of crystal & amber, opals & pearls
Taller & wiser than we were
Counted the day signs, the Bundle of Years
Opened the Book of Dreams, talked to the stars
Once they plucked from the wing of the sun
Chili-red araça, scarlet macaw, turquoise cotinga,

Black & gold troupial, gilded emerald-violet quetzal plumes
& once a giant bloodstone, blazing coal of night, flared over the city,
Plunged, hissing, into the lake

VERA CRUZ

Who are these men without pity from beyond the mist?
Howling like monkeys, lusting like pigs,
With great gray dogs, fire-mouthed, dripping saliva,
All in iron, blank & gleaming,
Plunging & turning, white eyes rolling,
Lathered & foaming they, galloping, galloped
Out of the bronze gong of the sun.
Thunder stick! Crack of black lightning!
Standing still, they kill at a distance,
Slaughter the sleeper in his dream at dawn.

COATLICUE

Salt Lady,
Elder sister of rain,
In your shift of yellow water lilies, billowing clouds,
Why are you weeping,
Weeping as you dance in the flowery field?

Under the churning grindstone,
Quern of stars,
Twittering like birds,
The poor glean in their blue cloaks
Scattered kernels of maize.

At the shattered gates,
Stone lips smeared with blood.

Delicatest hand of weaver, featherworker, goldsmith,
Smashed by the blunt iron fist.
Keepers of the Black House,
Bearing painted books of early spring—
Red heart of the red god flayed,
Torn apart by dogs.

Over the Place of No Exit,
Where the Jaguar Lord sits on his silver throne,
Iron hands raise the white stalk of
The God-Who-Has-Died.

XIPE TOTEC

naked before the night wind   drenched with flowers
darling adored one   the redteethed women
the milksquirting joyboys   perfumed pulque
sour maguey   *our lover*   morning glory seeds
peyote buds   *our brother*   flesh of sacred mushrooms
blue tobacco fumes   *our hero*   fires extinguished
what will you sell   from a distant hilltop
the pale sister   *your testicles*   morning star
your penis   her fiery brother   *your lips*
flowery branch   *your eyes*   bloodtipped broom
your ears   drifting clouds of butterflies   *your heart*
green quetzal plumes   *your tongue*   crowned with flowers
belled in gold   *earthshaker*   white chalk white feathers
ocelet-eared indigo-haired   *shapeshifter*   step by step
playing the flute you   *brave captive warrior*   climb
the slowly unfolding steps of time   *our lord*   at the apex
where four roads meet   *our enemy*   melting shapes rise & sink
swooning darkness   *our executioner*   jeweled hummingbirds
honey-dripping blossoms   *god of frost*   white bumblebees
dark calyx   *black axe*   milky bliss   *headless torso*

& squatting under the wetnurse tree   night mother   *who*
her left hand raised   *has given*   spreadeagled across stone
birth to   in the obsidian mirror   *the darkest sun*
the firedrill whirls   *where*   through goldringed fingers
are the five   out of the cobalt sky   *lost days*   the swordfish blade arcs
& plunges   hissing like smoke   *oldest god*   the bloodjet uncoils
over glistening stone   *god of the here*   who is it holds
& now   in trembling hands   *your red flower*
through the flayed mask of your own skin   *whose lips sing*

TENOCHTITLAN

Dreamreader of the Dreambook
How break the spell?

Lord of the Close & Near
For whom everything changes

Who will take it upon himself to be the sun,
Bring down the dawn?

Out of the dark catastrophe,
What golden afterglow?

Transparencies,
Veils of meaning?

Silence flowering
From the mouths of the dead?

What have we not said?
Who has not heard us?

What echoes back to us out of the mist?

H*T*L M*RQ**S

So the Frenchman confuses roses with vaginas,
silk umbrella with manta ray.
All we do is but the pale image of what we dream of doing.
A flashing wing.
Vico's flower turning turning in the sun.

Imprisoned in his tower,
M. le Six,
a debauched libertine & lucid reasoning being,
lectures on the decay of lying
from Cain's jawbone to the megaphone
& the new frisson—transparent as water over sand
rippling through the executioner's hand.

Today, the Observers of the Society of Man
present *homo ferus,* the wild child,
Victor,
V,
"the lost Dauphin."
Flushed by fox fires of the Revolution
from his savage solitude, the forests of Aveyron,
he's brought to justice by electric shocks from a Leyden jar,
taught to spell with heated metal letters pressed into his palm.
L-A-I-T he screams.
They roll him in the snowbanks of Rodez.

Bless the twice-born howling in the wind!
They've heard the whistle of the woodman's axe.

Crack a walnut. Fire a gun.
They startle, whimper, cringe.
They fear what grows out of them.
He shows them the root & flowering branch,
the hinge without the door,
saying, *The body is a threshold to be overcome!*

Supercilious light,
profil perdu, God's shadow
cast across the iron maiden of the bed,
"the obscene theater of sleep . . ."
As the red column falls
in a blizzard of black snow,
Floréal to Thermidor,
he sees the headless torso
& the flaming sword.
Ah, Saint-Just . . .
Darkest angel of our enlightenment . . .
Who stands between the guardian & the gate?
Who will watch the watchers of the State?

What is man? A jerk-off monkey?
Great Refusard
ejaculating giant figure 8s
across a shattered glass lake?
Intricate as Vaucanson's clockwork duck,
Leonardo's brazen-hearted lion,
the mirrored automata of the Turk,
this latest labor-saving device
(imp & engine of love's
perverse reversals,
reason's cul-de-sac),
severing head from heart
(*à la M. le docteur Guillotin*)
exposes public virtue's secret vice:

to wit, an ergonomically designed
perpetual motion pleasure machine,
viz., this wicker basket with wine-soaked wafer
fitted as bunghole for the Christmas goose
suspended by ratchets, harnesses, pulleys
triggered in a sequence of relays.
Now, take your novice, prelate, nun, &
arranging them (as in ill. 3) isoscelesed,
inserting *A* to *B* & *B* to *C* & *C* to *A*
until libido sparks—an anserine squawk—ergo . . .
Divine Afflatus? Golden Egg? Virgin Birth?
The moral of such post-Euclidian cupidity?
The Holy seeing what It lacks
finds even the Devil does God's work!
Thus, my Citizens, in Revolution's arsy-
varsy volte-face
crown serves as chamber pot.
Down the chain of sacred obligations
all's tried & true—tit
for twat—"noblesse oblige"
to the Golden Rule:
the doer doing does as s/he's been done to.
Hence, having thrashed the scullery maid,
I made 18 marks upon the mantel &
lowering my britches passed the rod to her.
This I call Spanish fly or
"making love with the whip hand."

May wine.
High postilion of the clouds.
Eros overruled, there is disorder in the polis.
Bordello of wild horses!
Sorcerers of wind!
Inside the pink-throated daffodil I see

a red groom buggering the Emperor's white swan.
Long live the miracle of the three-minute egg!
My incandescent blue lieutenants,
my drab-capped wrens,
my delicate dove of Venus, porcelain shoe,
my petite truffle moon mined by the snuffling swine of Perigord,
your mauve unfoldings, dark declivities,
your puckered apricot & indigo delta!
Where disgust is the footman of desire
what is the end of all our light & lust?
Sweet cruelty's delight?
A weasel in a rathole!

In truth, Madame,
you may as well prove to a pig
rosewater custard tastier than shit
as teach a fool to think or
hoodwink a whore into virtue.
Let others gorge & swill where weak appetite will
for the Man of Reason & true Libertine
freedom comes from following one's principles & pleasures.
Let the workmen laugh at you.
Obey my orders!
I want a top that screws
90 millimeters from the end,
a rosewood & ebony sheath,
cut glass inner flask
turned to my own measure for, as you know,
I have my reasons!
(Any good woman can tell you
when sheath comes loose in pocket, purse, etui
the surplus overflow too easily spills pell-mell,
all 6s, 9s,
'til your fair sex lies in mortal danger of

being pricked by pins & needles of an errant pleasure,
pain's petty recusals, brief resurrections,
sin's pretty little rosaries of an infant bliss.)

Send me also, posthaste,
crock of stewed pears, pot of Brittany butter,
3 doz. cherry gateaux of firmest texture
(not the dry-as-goat-turd tarts in your last batch),
orange blossom brandy, a bottle of *good* orgeat,
the pink taffeta hem torn from your loose gown,
3-ell-long green napkins,
6 doz. of M. Lenoir's night candles,
12 plump baby thrush wrapped in bacon fat ripe for the spit,
beef marrow pomade, the horsehair cushion with a hole,
the aforesaid sheath & cut glass dildo,
paper, pen, ink, per usual,
so I may single-handedly practice,
as they say, my *"vertu japonaise"*
& the following volumes: Toussaint's *Les Moeurs;*
Mystère d'Egypte; Réfutation de la Nature;
& *Bas-Empire,* in duodecimo.

Finally, here's a riddle fit for M. le Curé
& his brothel-keeper son,
the Honorable & Esteemed Archbishop of Lyons.
Once I had three children & a wife.
I was born in the bed my mother died in.
All night I held her in my arms.
Papa, Papa, she cried . . .
Now, Madame, let me iterate,
no threat or admonition of Church or State
can move me to deviate
from what I wish & what I will.
I'd pluck a quill from the dungiest swan,

dip it in Holy Virgin Blood
to write across the milky altar of each breast
my testament & philosophic faith:
Satisfy Thy Desires!
In closing, sweet Renée, nothing gives me greater pleasure
than to know thy pained heart
freely bound to one who remains as ever
your imprisoned Lord & Master,
M. de Sade.

LEVI'S STRAUS

When *Tel Quel*'s darling entertained
jackbooted sons & daughters of
the Emperor of Opera Hats,
Louis-Napoléon,
at the Socialist salon
in '68,
his razor wit guillotined
the thinking from the feeling part.
Constructing a frequency chart I found
the words most often employed:
langue, bouche, l'invisible
Lacan, libido, & *répétition*
which in super-Maoist semiotics
seems to mean
something like "rehearsal" as
the fiasco of '05
was a dress rehearsal for
the reversals of
'17.
Below, the rabble & the paving stones
inherited the street
while the Head of State ascended
loudspeakers in the trees,
choppers from a cloud
or disappeared into a maze
of Plexiglas visors, shields.
Behind teargas barricades
my Fulbright days & nights

overflowed with manifestos,
flesh-tinted pinups
of revolutionary whores & heroes,
color photos of napalm
& the atom bomb
until I couldn't tell ground zero from
vagina, ear, or anus
as I confessed, in a weak moment, to that prick,
von Kramm,
famous paperback & talk show advocate
of electroshock therapy
genitally applied
in the defense of the aggressive tendencies
of *homo capitalismus,* who is,
from my perspective as
participant-observer in the race,
an innately nasty creature
& a human worm.
Years later,
doing fieldwork in the Adirondacks
I discovered a puertorican pearldiver
flash his fire hose—*ca-rum-ba!*—
& one day reading *From Honey to Ashes* on the can
began an on-the-spot investigation into
the morphology of the hand
that blows the nose
& the hand that wipes
the shitty grin.

GHOST WARRIOR

Any time I walk into a place like this
I know I'm on the wrong side of the moon.
Eyes like lasers burning through me.
That spooky light off badly tuned TV.
I switch to auto, whip around.
There's smoke & whispers & that little click
as your assholes close. No, I don't want medals, Mister,
but I paid my dues. Two years in-country,
I never wasted anyone I didn't think was unfriendly.
Sure, sometimes there are flashes—black lightning,
my buddies sucking mud & everywhere
smell of a bar-b-que in Hell. My balls are brass,
my teeth freeze to ice cubes when I see
that candy-assed 2nd looey, old Golden Heel,
standing blue-eyed under fire.
Piece of metal whistles through his skull,
he's history. & those others,
my shadowboxing brothers-in-arms
rolling down waxed halls wall-to-wall & treetop tall
in their shiny Everest wheelchairs—ghost warriors.
So, when the doctors put the fear in my old lady & the kid,
I traded frag grenades, M16s, some ammo, a bazooka
for this rebuilt Harley Silver Shadow
with suicide shift on the left on account of the wires
in my hands, my knees. When it's cold, they burn like hell.
Then I wrote her a letter, saying, *Chill out baby.*
I love you to death . . . After the last lockup,
I dreamed a red moon, black grass, two pale oxen in a ville.

A voice said, *Vincent, be vigilant. Stay out of the sun.*
The night is a huge mirror you must look at.
I woke up & stared at my broken hands,
bags of old peanut shells, twisted sisters,
& thought, *What the fuck is my life, anyway?*
Next morning, I'm AWOL—a shadow flying
freaking bright light, 82nd Battalion's Albino Crow,
rocking wings, getting the monkey high!
Gliding across the black lake of the parking lot
in my Ray-Ban shades, purple-dyed snakeskin boots,
shirt of wild Hawaiian flowers, I'm *evil*—
an oil slick on asphalt. There's a *shimmer* in the air
& for a crazy second I'm out there, hanging in the glare,
almost invisible . . . Then I'm back in the black zipper sack
gagging on dog tags as I scream. The living nightmare!
What am I, Mister? Dead meat the body count missed?
Point on a ghost patrol? Crack open my skull, I tell the VA,
bet you'll find someone fucked with circuitry,
gray sponges soaking up dirty pictures, lies.
Fix me, I say, I'm yours, all yours.
A few jolts from the blue bolt, Mr. Screw & Dye's
just fine—a gen-u-ine made-in-the-shade
government-issue killing machine—except for dreams . . . bad dreams . . .

SHOAH

"Bitter, my friend, bitter? If you could lick my heart,
it would poison you."

Well, I'm a Jew who used to drink. I gave it up years ago
        after I had to leave Africa.
Call it "an unfavorable rate of exchange." As the joke goes,
        "It kills the pain."
In those days I'd sit in the dark, bottle of vodka in hand,
        reading Pascal's *Pensées*—
"What is the soul? Only a little wind & smoke?" until
        the *click* came.
I'd look out the trading post window & see the first gazelles
        wander down to the river.
It was like the dawn of creation—those gentle, elegant
        creatures
bending before salmon lilies, purple hyacinth, the cool,
        fire-reflecting waters,
& I'd say in my head, in Hebrew, the opening words of the
        Bible, *B'raishit*—"In the beginning . . ."
You know, I never realized until I said it just now—*B'raishit*—
        it's all shit, start to finish . . .

As my father, may he rest in peace, used to say—you know
        Yiddish?—I'll translate for you,
"Don't creep on that roof," meaning, There are some things
        best left alone.
Look too deeply, you see right through the rainbow to blinding
        white light & ashes . . .

No, for a Jew, wrestling all night with the darkest angels,
        limping home
under a diaspora of stars to build each day his temple,
        stone by stone,
stained by the blood of those who believed right to the end
        in false promises,
teeth gnawing on flesh, gnawing on bone, digging, digging
        the charpit of Babel,
for such a Jew, devoured, self-devouring, what is faith?
        "Fear of Night"?
"Fear of Not-Night"? The Great Refusals? For such a Jew, "No"
        is his "Yes"!
A synagogue of glass turned upside down on the table.

& what good is pity, my friend? Remorse? Or forgiveness?
        When we can never forget?
Just last night, closing my eyes in the dark, I saw the iron
        hood, glowing yellow lamp,
the cutthroat quarter-moon smile of the engineer. Soon I could
        hear the jackal-laugh
of the fireman shoveling coal, then the hiss of steam
        as slowly the cattle cars
rolled down blue rails toward the gleaming V—the *Rampe,*
        its Stone Queen,
& trailing behind in the stinking wind a stench even vodka
        can't kill,
squirming cesspool of blood & shit, those broken prayers
        for water, for air,
& now, gliding nearer, near, the terrible whispers—a whirring
        as of ashen wings,
as they, even they, the great sorrowful black-embered roses,
        opening, closing like silken bellows,
those Angels of Death in their moaning & weeping, their
        trembling lamentations,

fan, in their many-winged mourning & unearthly pity, higher,
    ever higher the flames . . .
Above, an immense arch opens to iron ports, & beyond,
    the grate—
behind which pulse flickering shadows—a faint white
    heartbeat of light . . .

When they abandoned us, I sat among smoldering corpses,
    sulfur fires,
those silver-cindered *Schwarzkommandos,* the ravens &
    crows,
staring at the burning night sky, where Venus hangs in the
    east, brightest
before it fades into the brightening, & said to myself, "I am
    the last Jew.
I'll wait for morning & the Germans . . ."

III

THE KEEPER OF RECORDS

for Raul Hilberg

Paper has been my business for over fifty years.
It began in an ex–torpedo factory outside Washington, D.C.,
a dusty windowless hive where as junior archivist
all day I read documents, mountains of captured documents.
Miles upon miles of paper to be filed in 40,000 linear feet of shelf.
Line after line, page after page. Slick blue-gray carbons,
crisp white originals. All filed in reverse chronological order
until the file is full & then put in a box & another file opened,
another file filled, & another & another & another,
& when the box is full you have a linear foot—thousands of documents.
They wanted me to read only about the Russians,
but I kept my eyes on the Jews, recording everything in my head,
letter by letter, number by number, line by line
unto the tenth generation light years away
so that even some minor clerk on the most distant star
might weep if he read this evidence of things unseen.

From the first, I could feel the force & uncanny precision,
the muted music of invisible machinery
as water is distilled by the limestone it runs through,
level by level, lock after lock, the whispering genius
of civil service that drives the wheel of that great mill,
pulverizing boulders into gravel, grinding difference down
to irreducible sameness. Even then I knew I must save
everything, everything must be accounted for
down to the last jot & tittle, so that nothing

be forgotten, no detail lost under the enormous inertia
& weight of trivia. For instance, a simple requisition to repair
a damaged rifle stock might be evidence of
the most brutal massacre. Scanning 1,000 frames of microfilm,
I came across a single line from Mariupol on the Black Sea,
a sentence biblical in its enormous brevity:
"Today, the security forces executed 8,000 Jews."
Everything you want to know in one sentence except . . .
Who can imagine what went on? Even imagining seems
a kind of obscenity. A man, a woman, a child—8,000 in all,
all standing on the beach before an open grave . . .
Do you really want to see them? (It turns out we have witnesses.)
They were naked (we are told), they were shivering, they asked for mercy.
They wept, they pleaded, they cried, they prayed.
They were broken down to, how shall I say, their essential elements.
& who were they facing under that blank sky?
Ah, the records, the payroll, allow us to identify them.
I could read you the roster of those security forces,
the names of the dutiful men now long dead, or dying.
I could even tell you what uniforms they wore, what insignia,
the well-drilled way they responded to orders,
the sharp commands, & then the spasms—flame, thunder, & smoke,
the recoil into silence before it all starts again,
round after round after round rolling down the line
like some crazy clockwork, mad mesh of gears,
as one by one by one the bodies, twisted, gesturing, fall
into the ditch. Do you really want the details?
After all, it is just another day's work. You think it is easy
doing what they do? They are breathing heavily,
wiping sweat from their eyes. They take a break. Give time
for the overheated barrels to cool. Someone
strikes a match on a boot, lights a cigarette
in his cupped, trembling hand, another stares at a gull
wheeling out of the ragged heart of the sun.

There is a whimper, a moan. One of them leans over the ditch,
raises his rifle, brings it down with a hollow thud
on a rotten pumpkin, bald skull. & behind them all, amid blood & smoke,
stands a bespectacled man, notebook in hand. What is he doing?
Why he is counting the bodies, accounting for the expense of time,
waste of materiel, bullet after bullet after bullet after bullet
down to the final pfennig. Perhaps he is the same man
who sits at his desk later that night wearily writing
the requisition for the damaged rifle, & typing that perfunctory,
summary sentence: *"Today, the security forces . . ."*

O, my friends, there are puzzles & mysteries
even in the most complete, the most logical accounting.
Double entries to the God of Solitude & Locked Doors.
The railways, for instance. They fascinated me.
On the surface, what could be simpler, more routine.
So many pfennigs per person per kilometer of track.
Timetables of trains that will not leave, none of them,
without passengers, & all of them going one way, one way!
Yet it takes great ingenuity & skill to manage
that complicated network of railways, the iron web,
its stockyards, switching stations, shunts & arteries,
its carefully calibrated interconnecting systems of
one-way trips spread all across Europe,
shuttling back & forth, back & forth
from daylight to darkness to daylight again,
picking up, along the way, "units" of freight,
invoices, exit visas, each duly noted,
numbered, documented in duplicate, triplicate:
Macedonian miner, Viennese music teacher, tailor from Salonika . . .
Why it took me ten years to figure out what
the number 33 meant, & years more before I could decipher
the color-coded red/green/blue pencil marks.
What is saved? What lost? Of course, we make mistakes,

we are human, we err. There is a slip of the pen,
documents misfiled, we become victims of some vandal
allied hand. There are monstrous misinterpretations,
false keys, repressed doubts; still one keeps faith,
knowing all the time because it doesn't mean one thing
doesn't mean it means nothing, knowing all the time
that even amid the most casual, the coldest calculations
nothing is lost, nothing wasted, knowing all the time
it would take a book twenty times larger
than the largest phone book simply to record the names,
just the names, of the Jews, the dead Jews;
& always the search for that pale, precise man
who understands trains, the nightmare bureaucrat
who, perhaps, means no one harm, seeks proper authorization
for what was never spelled out, the man with all the strands in his hands—
the spider-God. For years I have shadowed him across Europe,
admired in a strange way his fidelity to fact, his demonic
attention to detail, the clever unknotting of unforeseen complications
as hour after hour he keeps to his schedule. So one continues,
the evidence mounts; more than hearsay, witnesses,
the statistics tell their own cruel, neutral tale,
a tale that would turn a trial lawyer's hair white overnight!
& still he sits at his desk, my counterpart, *mein Schattenbruder.*
He never moves, he is patient, painstaking,
he follows the logic that leads from one thing to another,
he never looks up as he plots the long intricate passage
from darkness to light to darkness again.

What am I looking for? Codes? Ciphers? Signals?
Columns of symbols? Random marks on a page?
Here is one—gray/black dots—an air reconnaissance photo.
From this height you can see the pure geometry of buildings
laid out in rows, metal roofs where body heat
has melted the snow. & wavering in winter air?

The time frame matched with internal memos
helps us pinpoint that thin worm trail
as a group of Jews newly arrived from Posen
marching single file toward the shadow-gate,
its wisp of smoke, the murder mill at Birkenau.
& this one, stamped <u>CONFIDENTIAL</u>. Let me translate.
"& Himmler said to them: *In this most narrow circle,*
we must face the hard demands of what is not easily spoken.
To make a whole people disappear from the earth,
men, women, yes, even children unto the tenth generation,
to do the hard thing & remain decent.
Who does not know a decent Jew?
But now 50 bodies, 500, 5,000 . . .
To do the hard thing . . .
This never to be written page in our glorious history."
Who has the last word? The first? My task is only
to repay my debts, give credit where credit is due,
leave the book open for all to read what is brought to light.
In the beginning, I say, *In the beginning . . .*

THE GATE OF HORN

Forgive me if I seem a bit at sea
but you woke me from a dream of words
I was setting to music I'll want you
to transcribe for me—a quatrain Shakespeare wrote
when he was eleven, "The uncertain glory
of an April day." At my age, what is life
but a *recitativo oscuro,* with its shadowy intimations,
musical aphorisms, librettos in a sigh.
Caught between willful tempestuousness
& bewildering geometries, we dread & long for
those moments of cruel lucidity that fix us as we are—
   Mallarmé's swan
frozen in ice . . .
      Last night I sat here alone in the dark
listening to the overture of the coming storm—distant rumbling
like sheet metal rolling off a giant press, then the true
cacophony, a delirium of lightning bolts, thunderclaps,
whiff of ozone in charged air—as though nature's wunderkind—
"a lion flayed alive"—drove a lyric electric concert grand
hurtling over Niagara Falls. As my kinsman,
that half-caste past master of the hyperclimactic
molto grandioso crescendo, Beethoven,
reminds us, "The world is king," & we but paupers,
doing its bidding. Staring out the window in the rain
I could feel time passing like a wall of moving mirrors,
a river in which is reflected the wing of evening
speckled with stars, & thought, *Night sky, whose mind are you?*

The stars, the stars are inside our heads. & now
out of the silence the dead rising: ghosts of Buffalo soldiers
& Oglala Sioux—winged messengers—like great blue herons
arrowing over the lake where the black spring lambs gambol,
late for the sacrifice . . .
                              After the storm,
I followed the tone rows & tentative *tap tap tap*
of drainpipe off metal roof—a blind man's cane, wandering
Oedipus—sensations uprooted to atmospheric effects,
the many weathers of this moment, this place,
its windy gusts, fleeting moods, scherzo of cloud shadow
racing over rock face, & wondered, at the risk of forgetfulness,
where do we go, venturing forth beyond our murky
origins? Recapture against failing light
memories of a rusted harrow leaning upon
a dusky barn door, a swaybacked horse the color of "bricks
wrapped in silk," thunder of boots on a hardwood floor,
& smell once more that starched white linen apron
we buried our eyes in. I hate farewells, don't you?
& the terror of coming back to what is at once new
& familiar, a reunion of two times chimed exactly
that leaves us estranged from ourselves, staring at shadows
trembling in the shade. What will save us? Who appear
at the head of our bed announcing, "Cast off your shackles
& chains!" & place in our hands the sacred instruments,
show us the great tablets scriven in the sky,
prophesying, "These are the road signs to Heaven
& gateways to the Pearly Everlasting!" & looking up
we shall see on high the letters & the numbers, the figures
of all the creatures of the Lord, all carved in the frozen music
of stone—the Lion lying down with the Lamb, the Oriole
serenading the lowly Mule at dawn, the Dove fanning
the Night Nurse's brow, the three Angels washing the feet
of the weary Day Laborer, & His Son come down in a cloud at last
to lift the veil . . .

Do raise the shade—& fill that glass.
Ah, whiskey is a great river . . . Is that a sunspot or a swan? . . .
What do I miss most at my age? . . .
Seeing the stars.

NOTES

"The Widows of Gravesend" is indebted to the storyteller Gioia Timpanelli and quotes from letters of Charles Olson.

"The Waters of Time" is a phrase of Martin Heidegger's.

"Dies Irae" was inspired by and occasionally cites Robert Kaplan's marvelous book *The Nothing That Is: A Natural History of Zero.*

"House of the Fifth Sun" draws from Inga Clendinnen's magisterial study, *Aztecs.*

"H*t*l M*rq**s" quotes from Neil Schaeffer's translations of the letters of Marquis de Sade.

green
press
INITIATIVE

Northwestern University Press is committed to preserving ancient forests and natural resources. We elected to print this title on 30% post consumer recycled paper, processed chlorine free. As a result, for this printing, we have saved:

1 Trees (40' tall and 6-8" diameter)
631 Gallons of Wastewater
1 Million BTUs of Total Energy
38 Pounds of Solid Waste
131 Pounds of Greenhouse Gases

Northwestern University Press made this paper choice because our printer, Thomson-Shore, Inc., is a member of Green Press Initiative, a nonprofit program dedicated to supporting authors, publishers, and suppliers in their efforts to reduce their use of fiber obtained from endangered forests.

For more information, visit www.greenpressinitiative.org

Environmental impact estimates were made using the Environmental Defense Paper Calculator. For more information visit: www.papercalculator.org.